a boy's guide to **Heavenly Mother**

By McArthur Krishna & Martin Pulido
With contributions by Bethany Brady Spalding

Art by: Allen Tenbusschen, Amber Eldredge, Ashly S. Correia, Brooke Bowen, Colby Adams Sanford, Clint Whiting, Crystal Suzanne Close, David Cassler, David Habben, Del Parson, Elizabeth Sanchez, Emilie Buck Lewis, Haylee NgÐroma Solomon, Heather Ruttan, Howard Lyon, J. Kirk Richards, Lisa Aerin Collett, Lexi Lyon, Linda V. Etherington, Lisa Jensen, Megan Schaugaard, Rose Datoc Dall, Rebecca Everett, Rick Shorten, Sage Gallagher, Samuel Walker, Shari Lyon, Stephanie Northrup

Glorious thanks to the many LDS artists who have generously shared their vision of Heavenly Mother.

D Street PRESS

Dear Parents,

A former presiding bishop, Elder John H. Vandenberg, once observed: "Your life is not really your own. It was given to you by your earthly parents, as well as by your heavenly parents." We didn't call ourselves into existence. Our creation was an act of grace.

Anyone introduced to economics has heard, "There ain't no such thing as a free lunch," conveying that all choices have opportunity costs. And yet, while buying tickets to a sports game may keep us from the movies, one event can be considered the ultimate free lunch: our birth. In coming from others, there was no cost, no alternative lost. With birth, our Heavenly Parents gave us the possibility of having any possibilities. This is a gift we can neither reject nor repay. There is no act we can give our Heavenly Father and Heavenly Mother that is reciprocal to this.

Nonetheless, humans can live in awareness of the fundamental generosity of existing, reverencing our Heavenly Parents, which "in the first place...hath created [us], and granted unto [us our] lives, for which [we] are indebted" (Mosiah 2:23). It's no surprise that church rituals like baptism or a navel mark in sacred clothing remind us of birth. For birth tells us right away that human life is deeply relational, one of heritages and inheritances and roles. All relationships are to be handled with care. From this stems the ancient commandment, "Honor thy father and thy mother," which was written by God on tablets of stone (Exodus 20:12). The prophet Russell M. Nelson has clarified, "Honor not only your earthly parents, but your Heavenly Parents as well" (*Friend*, Jan. 1986).

To honor our Heavenly Parents, we must get to know Them, understand Their work, serve Them, and reverence Them, even as we forge our own lives and sometimes disappoint Their expectations. But most often our life adventures delight Them, adding to a beautiful cosmos They judged to be good at creation's dawn.

This guidebook is designed to aid boys and young men—our sons or nephews or those boys we love—in adopting a life of gratitude by helping them recognize the infinite grace in their birth. It will particularly help them know their Heavenly Mother, their relationship to Her as sons, and their relationship to Her daughters (their sisters). This book can help them reflect on the wondrous opportunities mortality provides them. It will encourage actions that lead them to grow closer to Heavenly Mother and Heavenly Father, and Their Son Jesus Christ, so that they feel Their love and become like Them—the ultimate joy.

— Martin

What you'll find inside A Boy's Guide to Heavenly Mother

This guide is filled with truths, tips, quotes, questions, activities, and amazing art to help you:

↖ Artist: Amber Eldridge, *Mother of All*

KNOW YOUR HEAVENLY MOTHER... AND YOURSELF!

#1 United to be God
#2 Equal in might and glory
#3 Shares godly traits
#4 Perfectly loving parent
#5 Eternal influencer
#6 Creator

UNDERSTAND MARVELOUS TRUTHS ABOUT YOUR LIFE

#1 You have a moral responsibility
#2 You have eternal relationships
#3 You have a matriarchal line
#4 You have an ultimate female role model
#5 You have the gift of Her Son

CREATE CHANGE FOR A MORE LOVING WORLD

#1 In yourself
#2 In your family
#3 In your church community
#4 Throughout the whole world

TO ALL THE BOYS IN THE WORLD:

Boys that kick a soccer ball, play in mud, enjoy a video game, pretend (or know) they are superheroes, build Legos, code on computers, read and write novels, scribble cartoons, buzz into a trumpet or pluck a guitar, work on farms, learn at schools, surf, go on dates, and beyond...

As you mature and feel the excitement and the weight of responsibility of becoming a man, here are three key principles that can strengthen and guide you:

1 You are a son of Heavenly Mother and Heavenly Father, whose love and tender concern for you never ends. You are never alone.

2 Within you is a spark from God, a seed of divinity.

3 You have the potential to grow in goodness, knowledge, and joy through the Atonement of Jesus Christ. Your Heavenly Parents want you to reach your full potential—**to be as They are**.

Every day of your life's journey, let these truths uplift you and inspire you to know what to do next. Rejoice that you are a beloved son of Heavenly Parents.

LEARN ABOUT THEM—SO YOU CAN BECOME MORE LIKE THEM!

1. Psalm 82:6; Job 38:7

2. Doctrine and Covenants 93:19–20, 29, 33

3. Luke 2:52; Hebrews 5:8; Matthew 5:48; 3 Nephi 12:48

Artist: Lisa Aerin Collett, *Creating the Universe*

Artist: Howard Lyon, *Prima Luce Caelesti*

LET'S LEARN ABOUT HEAVENLY MOTHER…AND YOU!

Because you are a child of Heavenly Parents, **you** have a "divine nature and destiny."* But what is your divine destiny? President Dallin H. Oaks said it straight: "Our theology begins with heavenly parents. Our highest aspiration is to be like them."

Theology means the study of God. "Our highest aspiration" is the same as saying **THE GOAL** of earth life is to become like our Heavenly Parents. But what are They like?

Lots of places teach you about Heavenly Father, so this book focuses on **Heavenly Mother**. Let's learn about Her!

66 We, the human family, [are] literally the sons and daughters of divine Parents, the spiritual progeny of God our Eternal Father, and of our God Mother. 99

– Elder James E. Talmage

66 This glorious vision of life hereafter, revealed by the Prophet of the Restoration, is given radiant warmth by the thought that among the exalted beings in the world to come we shall find a mother who possesses the attributes of Godhood. 99

– Elder John A. Widtsoe

*"The Family: A Proclamation to the World," *Ensign*, Nov. 2010, 129.

UNITED TO BE GOD

Heavenly Mother and Heavenly Father are UNITED. In fact, only together are Father and Mother fully divine. Think about this—you can't be divine by yourself! When you are united, you are one with someone—which is different from being the same. It is working as one **two-gether**.

Can you think of things our Heavenly Parents might have worked on as a team? Beyond galactic superclusters, the Blood Falls of Antarctica, or the barreleye deep-sea fish, how about the plan of happiness? According to President M. Russell Ballard, "We are part of a divine plan designed by Heavenly Parents who love us." It's the plan to help us grow on earth and return to Them someday—that's important work to do together!

Regardless if you marry, it is necessary for men and women to learn to work together.

66 [In Genesis] we are informed that it required the male and female, united, to make one image of [God's] own body... It required the male and female to make an image of God. 99

– Elder Franklin D. Richards

66 I testify there is no greater goal in mortality than to live eternally with our Heavenly Parents and our beloved Savior, the Lord Jesus Christ. But it is more than just our goal—it is also Their goal. They are totally, completely, eternally aligned with us. 99

– President M. Russell Ballard

 As you read about God in the scriptures, can you imagine Heavenly Mother and Heavenly Father joined together?

THINK OF PEOPLE IN YOUR LIFE: YOUR PARENTS, YOUR BROTHERS AND SISTERS, YOUR FRIENDS. HOW ARE YOU UNITED WITH THEM? HOW ARE YOU NOT? WHAT KEEPS YOU FROM BEING UNIFIED? HOW CAN YOU IMPROVE?

Artist: Megan Schaugaard, *Heavenly Parents*

Artist: Heather Ruttan, *God the Mother*

EQUAL IN MIGHT & GLORY

As a Goddess, Heavenly Mother is **equal** in might and glory to Heavenly Father!

DIVINE ATTRIBUTE #2

 "The divine Mother, side by side with the divine Father, [has] the **equal** sharing of **equal** rights, privileges and responsibilities." Susa Young Gates

EQUALITY IS DIVINE.
How awesome is that?

Heavenly Mother and Heavenly Father work side by side to love and bless Their children. They partner joyously together, generating love that expands the universe—literally creating worlds without end. Our Heavenly Parents are a perfect example of equal partnership.

 IF EQUALITY IS DIVINE, WHAT CAN YOU DO TO SEE AND TREAT OTHERS AS EQUALS?

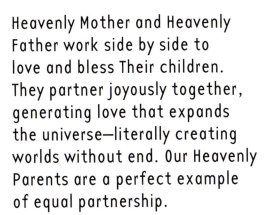

66 No matter to what heights God has attained or may attain, he does not stand alone; for side by side with him, in all her glory, a glory like unto his, stands a companion, the Mother of his children. For as we have a Father in heaven, so also we have a Mother there, a glorified, exalted, ennobled Mother. 99

– Elder Melvin J. Ballard

SHARES GODLY TRAITS

Heavenly Mother and Heavenly Father share godly characteristics. The *Encyclopedia of Mormonism* says She is like Him "in glory, perfection, compassion, wisdom, and holiness." ⟿⟶

In the Hebrew language in the Old Testament, one word for God—*Elohim*—is actually plural. Elohim = Gods! Notice how in Joseph Smith's translation of the Book of Abraham, the story of Creation always mentions "the Gods" (see Abraham 3–5). So the word *God* in the Old Testament can sometimes refer to both Heavenly Parents.

As part of God, Heavenly Mother has divine attributes. The scriptures teach:

- God can reach you anywhere
  (see Jeremiah 23:23–24).

- God knows all the details: the scriptures say They even count the hairs on your head...don't you think They also know of your worries and dreams? (see Luke 12:7).

- God creates infinite worlds and fills them with all kinds of life
  (see Moses 1:37; Genesis 1–2).

- God loves us deeply, shown perfectly through sending Jesus Christ
  (see Psalm 145:8; 1 John 3:11; 1 John 1:5).

In addition to scripture, modern revelation teaches us of Heavenly Mother's attributes and mission too. We know that She and Heavenly Father are almighty, surpassingly intelligent, and **omnipotent**.

Look up the amazing scriptures when God is described as a woman: *"You were unmindful of the Rock that bore you; you forgot the God who gave you birth"* (Deuteronomy 32:18). Or, *"Can a woman forget her nursing child, or show no compassion for the child of her womb? Even these may forget, yet I will not forget you"* (1 Nephi 21:15).

Artist:
Clint Whiting,
Arms Wide

Artist:
Samuel Walker,
Lead, Carry, Follow

66 I pray that you and I will never forget sacred eternal truths—first and foremost that we are sons and daughters of living and loving Heavenly Parents, who desire only our eternal happiness. 99

– Elder Ronald A. Rasband

PERFECTLY LOVING PARENT

DIVINE ATTRIBUTE #4

Another thing your Heavenly Parents share is **YOU**. You are Their child. You are loved perfectly by Them. Your Heavenly Parents love you no matter what you do or say. Heavenly Mother and Heavenly Father *are* love. →

 1 John 4:8

And loving parents teach their kids (and tease them a little too)! Our Heavenly Parents set up earth life like a school to help us learn to be more like Them. So, They help us—and push us—to overcome our weaknesses. Heavenly Mother and Heavenly Father knew that even with our best efforts, we would not be perfect, so They sent Jesus Christ to atone for us. When we get stuck, we can be reassured that They can *absolutely* guide us through our human challenges.

Being our Heavenly Parents is Their main job—They will **ALWAYS** help!

 "A basic gospel principle is that we are children of loving Heavenly Parents. It is only natural for Them to help us in every way to return to our heavenly home." – Elder Gary E. Stevenson

They loved us first, and true joy lies in loving Them back. → 1 John 4:19

66 He [Heavenly Father] and your Mother in heaven value you beyond any measure. **99**
– President Spencer W. Kimball

WHEN HAVE YOU FELT MOST LOVED BY YOUR HEAVENLY MOTHER? WHAT HAVE YOU DONE TO SHOW YOU LOVE HER BACK?

Artist:
David Habben,
Matriarch

ETERNAL INFLUENCER

Heavenly Mother and Heavenly Father have been with us from the beginning, and They will continue with us throughout eternity. Just think—while we develop and become more like Them, we never outgrow Them! We can always turn to Them.

 We will *always* need Them.

The Apostle Orson F. Whitney taught, "But what about the eternal Father and Mother? Have they no claim upon us? Why should we not return to them, and resume the relations of the previous life?"

Our Heavenly Mother and Heavenly Father are not just heavenly parents—They are our **eternal parents**. They will guide our destinies forever. There is no end to the adventures we may go through together!

ACTIVITY

How can you recognize our Heavenly Mother's influence in your life? Record you thoughts and feelings here.

_____ _____

_____ _____

_____ _____

_____ _____

_____ _____

_____ _____

_____ _____

CREATOR

Our Heavenly Parents are both **creators**. Not only did They bring our spirits into being, but the whole world that surrounds us. Heavenly Mother is a co-creator of spirits, raging rivers, mountain peaks, stars, and worlds without end.*

But, guess what? We can be like Them—we can grow in our creative capacities too! In fact, all of us can create now on this earth. Think how you can influence the world with your talents.

- Building things as simple as Legos and blanket forts, or as complex as homes and computer code, or as beautiful as temples and gardens.

- Composing songs, paintings, poems, or dances.

- Shaping visions of unseen worlds by writing stories, comics, or films.

- Forging friendships, communities, and marriages.

- Creating jobs so others have a livelihood.

Your Heavenly Parents have entrusted you with **creative powers to shape this universe** with Them. Every day you can create!

66 In the ongoing process of creation—our creation and the creation of all that surrounds us—our heavenly parents are preparing a lovely tapestry with exquisite colors and patterns and hues. They are doing so lovingly and carefully and masterfully. And each of us is playing a part—our part—in the creation of that magnificent, eternal piece of art. 99

– Sister Patricia Holland

*See Moses 1:33, 37–38; Ezekiel 11:19–20; 2 Corinthians 5:17

WHAT IS SOMETHING YOU'VE MADE THAT YOU ARE PROUD OF? WHAT MAKES IT SPECIAL? HOW DOES IT MAKE YOU GOD-LIKE?

Artist:
Sage Gallagher,
They Sent Their Son

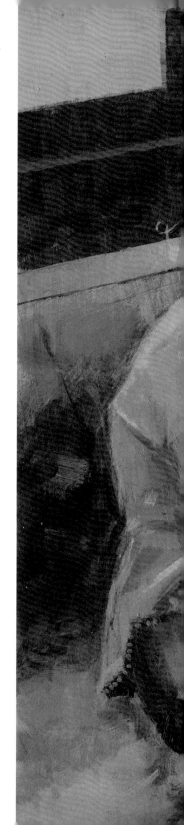

WHAT DOES THIS ALL MEAN FOR YOU?

Now you know a lot about our Heavenly Parents. Just as Heavenly Mother and Heavenly Father have partnered together, **They want to partner with you** too. Did you know that's the primary reason you're here on earth? They are giving you countless opportunities to refine yourself, to help you see who you are, and to choose who you wish to become.

LET'S EXPLORE MORE! WHAT MARVELOUS TRUTHS ARE INHERENTLY PART OF YOUR MORTAL LIFE EXPERIENCE? AND, WHAT ARE THE TOOLS OUR HEAVENLY PARENTS HAVE GIVEN TO HELP YOU ALONG THE WAY? KEEP READING...

YOU HAVE A MORAL RESPONSIBILITY

You proved faithful to our Heavenly Parents while in heaven.* Now you have the amazing opportunity of earth life!

Like a cartoon flipbook, each day of your life is a page, a little slice of time. As you go about facing challenges, **your choices will determine who you become**. This life is your soul in motion. You are showing yourself and your Heavenly Parents if you are ready to partner with Them on the next step...and the next step...and the next.

So how do you show you are ready to partner with Them?

- You can use your agency to freely choose the good.

- You can care for your body.

- You can resist selfish impulses and consider others' needs too.

- You can be a wise steward over yourself and the earth.

These are ENORMOUS responsibilities—but our Heavenly Parents know we can succeed!

> 66 The primary purposes of our existence upon the earth are to obtain a body of flesh and bones, to gain experience that could come only through separation from our heavenly parents, and to see if we would keep the commandments. 99
> – President Thomas S. Monson

 Artist: Crystal Suzanne Close, *A Heavenly Mother's Love*

LIFE TIP:

Think of temptations as a mirror. Temptations are constant and give you a way to see who you are—and how you can improve. One of Jesus's disciples was Peter. He was called the Rock. Peter thought he would never deny Jesus, but later he did (see Matthew 26:73–75). Why is this story important? It shows us that when we make mistakes and fail, we can learn and repent. Peter changed—becoming a valiant Apostle! (Read the book of Acts to learn more.)

*See Abraham 3:22–28.

YOU HAVE ETERNAL RELATIONSHIPS

Our Heavenly Parents have created the opportunity for developing new relationships here on earth:

- Right now, you're learning to build relationships with your family as a son, grandson, or maybe a brother.

- When you're older, you can continue learning about relationships through dating.

- If you marry, treat your spouse as you think Heavenly Father would treat Heavenly Mother.

- Whether you are a biological father, adopt, or act as a father figure for others in need—being a father is divine.

Fatherhood, guardianship, and marriage enable you to live like our Heavenly Parents—**family life is the divine life!** (Even when it can feel tough).

Relationships are the structure of both this mortal life and celestial life. Relationships MATTER! They are the center of human and divine identity, purpose, potential, and aspiration. If you want to be like your Heavenly Parents, strive to care about your relationships like They do.

 Your mortal body possesses the AMAZING ability to generate life. Treat your body, others' bodies, and sex as sacred.

WHAT ARE YOUR MOST VALUED RELATIONSHIPS, AND WHY?
HOW CAN YOU NURTURE THOSE RELATIONSHIPS NOW?

Artist: Rebecca Everett, *Hope and Promise*

LIFE TIP: You can create divine relationships in all places. You can learn to be a good friend to classmates at school. When you get a job, you can be a supportive coworker. Church service provides opportunities to build relationships by connecting and caring for others as a priesthood holder, a full-time missionary, or a ministering brother.

> To all of our mothers everywhere, past, present, or future, I say, 'Thank you. Thank you for giving birth, for shaping souls, for forming character, and for demonstrating the pure love of Christ.' To Mother Eve, to Sarah, Rebekah, and Rachel, to Mary of Nazareth, and to a Mother in Heaven, I say, 'Thank you for your crucial role in fulfilling the purposes of eternity.'
>
> – Elder Jeffrey R. Holland

Artist: J. Kirk Richards, *Divine Lineage*

YOU HAVE A MATRIARCHAL LINE

MARVELOUS TRUTH #3

Did you know you belong to a long line of mothers and fathers? If you can, find photos of your ancestors, and bring them to a mirror. Notice the similarities between yourself and your foremothers and forefathers. It might be in your eye color, the shape of your nose, or the waviness of your hair. Then notice your clothing and the home surrounding you. Think of the language you speak, your education, and the activities you enjoy. Remember that so much of your life comes from the contributions and efforts of your ancestors.

When you're ordained as an elder, you may be shown your priesthood lineage—how your priesthood line traces back to Jesus. But, don't forget **you also have a matriarchal lineage** tracing back to your Heavenly Mother.

Among these mothers, you might find painters, midwives, pioneers, felt hat workers, teachers, ranchers, businesswomen. They braved voyages across oceans and treks across plains, endured wars, participated in revolutions, suffered inequalities, danced to fiddles, and found their joys. Many risked their lives bringing children into the world. Learn from them how to navigate a course through your own life.

Value the women you came from—including your Heavenly Mother!

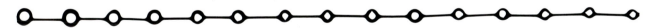

66 Women are endowed with special traits and attributes that come trailing down through eternity from a divine mother. 99

– Elder Vaughn J. Featherstone

ACTIVITY

See the Generational Chart on page 48 of this guide book. Think of what you owe your foremothers and how they reflect the love and attributes of your Heavenly Mother.

YOU HAVE AN ULTIMATE FEMALE ROLE MODEL

It may feel like a long way off now, but, sometime, you will think about who you want to date and who you want to marry. And when you consider that, you should think of **Heavenly Mother**...She is an ultimate role model!

Heavenly Mother and Heavenly Father are equal partners. You need an equal partner too! Since you know about Heavenly Mother, you know to choose someone who is strong, who has good ideas, and who wants to **work together** on achieving shared goals. Just remember, no matter what else, you want to choose someone who loves and serves our Heavenly Parents.

As you're raising your family together, **strive to be united** with your spouse. You can encourage their growth and development, just as they encourages yours. You can become a divine TEAM—just like our Heavenly Parents.

> 66 Mormon theology gives no less glorious origin, or less high destiny to woman. If it teaches that man is the Son of God, it teaches also that woman is the daughter of God; if it teaches that in the great future men will become kings and priests unto God, it teaches also that women will become queens and priestesses...To one accepting 'Mormon' theology, the sexes are not made to walk separately and alone... Neither one can say to the other, 'I have no need of thee!' 99
>
> – Elder B. H. Roberts

LIFE TIP:
Along the way, learn to treat women with greater respect. Learn to listen to them. Learn to value them. They are your equals in might and glory. Treat them as you think Heavenly Mother would want to be treated.

Artist: Rose Datoc Dall, *Worlds Without Number*

66 I live to teach my boys to be content with themselves and life as it comes to them, and to reverence womanhood as the joint jewel which adorns the dual crown of Heavenly Parentage. 99
– Susa Young Gates

HOW DOES KNOWING ABOUT OUR HEAVENLY MOTHER CHANGE HOW YOU TREAT THE GIRLS IN YOUR LIFE?

YOU HAVE THE GIFT OF HER SON

Our Heavenly Parents gave us the **ultimate gift** of Their enduring love by sending Their Son to earth. Can you even begin to imagine how hard it was for Heavenly Mother to be separated from Jesus? She watched Him be treated with cruelty and ultimately be crucified. That must have been heartwrenching. But She loves YOU enough that She was willing to bear watching Jesus suffer.

Heavenly Mother knew that the work Jesus would do on this earth was essential. Jesus leads us back to our Heavenly Parents! Heavenly Mother knew her Son Jesus could show us the way by being a perfect example. Jesus would have the chance to gain a body, like us. He would have the chance to be tempted, like us. And He would have the chance to choose His Parents' plan, like us. Jesus would show us that you can suffer from evil and not become evil. Mortal life is hard, but through Jesus **we can triumph** over its challenges.

And what does all this mean?

MARVELOUS TRUTH #5

66 Jesus is our Savior and Redeemer, and His restored gospel will lead us safely back to the presence of our Heavenly Parents. 99

– President M. Russell Ballard

66 I testify of that grand destiny, made available to us by the Atonement of the Lord Jesus Christ, who Himself continued 'from grace to grace' until in His immortality He received a perfect fullness of celestial glory. I testify that in this and every hour He is, with nail-scarred hands, extending to us that same grace, holding on to us and encouraging us, refusing to let us go until we are safely home in the embrace of Heavenly Parents. 99

–Elder Jeffrey R. Holland

Artist: Del Parson, *Heavenly Mother*

LIFE TIP:

Show your gratitude for your Heavenly Mother by following Her Son—They both want us to grow and develop.

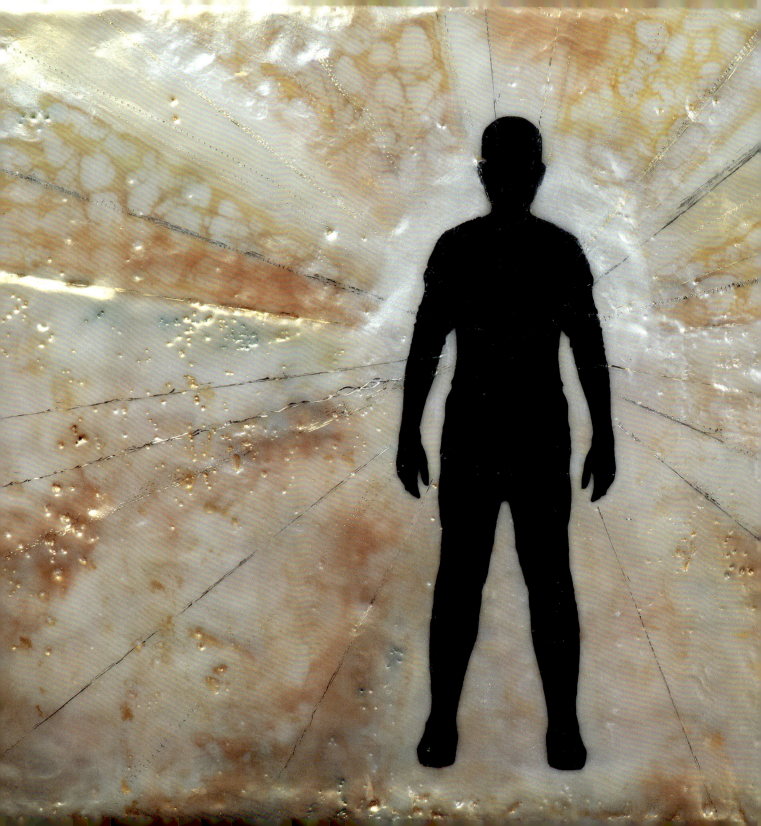

President John Taylor described your potential so powerfully:

66 He is a God in embryo, and possesses within him a spark of that eternal flame which was struck from the blaze of God's eternal fire in the eternal world, and is placed here upon the earth that he may possess true intelligence, true light, true knowledge,—that he may know himself—that he may know God. 99

JUST THINK,
YOU ARE A GOD!
IN THE MAKING

Artist: Shari Lyon, *Sparks of Divinity*

TURNING TRUTH INTO ACTION

Artist: Rick Shorten, *Heavenly Parents*

66 It is not enough that theology helps me to understand God. It must also help me to understand myself and my world. 99

– Francine R. Bennion

Wow. We have covered a lot of truths so far. But knowing is not enough. Now you have to take action. So what do you do with all of these truths you've discovered in this guidebook?

(PSSST: KEEP READING— THERE ARE TIPS AHEAD!)

IN YOURSELF

Knowing your Heavenly Parents **can change who you are.** You change as you seek to know Them and Their will in your life. You already pray to your Heavenly Father. How can you include Heavenly Mother in your life?

Write your own ideas here:

_____

_____

_____

_____

_____

_____

_____

_____

ACTIVITY

Learn more of your Heavenly Mother. Lots of prophets and apostles have spoken of Her. You can see their words throughout this whole book, but there are lots more! Go to the Activity Pages starting on page 46 and ponder more scriptures, and go check out SeekingHeavenlyMother.com to see a bunch of quotes, poems, art, essays, and more.

TOP 10 IDEAS

1. Try to recognize Heavenly Mother's influence in your life.

2. Be grateful for all that She has done for you.

3. Be mindful of Her as you read the scriptures.

4. Hang artwork in your room that reminds you of Her.

5. Think of Her during church services.

6. Meditate on the gift of Her Son.

7. Keep a journal of when you feel Her love.

8. Treat girls and women as Her daughters.

9. Practice equality.

10. Value people who are different than you.

Artist: Lexi Lyon, *A Gentle Correction*

> **“** Let love abound among you; be one family, let there be no [contention], but know that you have one father and mother in the eternal heaven where all is peace and love. **”**
>
> – Elder David C. Kimball

Artist:
Elizabeth Sanchez,
Nearby Mother

 **CREATE CHANGE #2**

IN YOUR FAMILY

You can use truths about Heavenly Mother to strengthen your own family in different ways.

1. RESPECT YOUR EARTHLY MOTHER

In addition to helping you with your homework and cheering you on at your events, your mother can get revelation, lead, and make decisions—she is in your life to help you. She's likely **known and loved you** longer than you've known yourself; her perspective is invaluable.

2. PRACTICE DIVINE EQUALITY IN YOUR HOME

Appreciate when you see parents demonstrating partnership—they're showing you a model of how our Heavenly Parents act! But what can you do in your family? Are you and your siblings equally sharing the responsibilities and fun of family life? Are you listening to both your mother and your father's guidance? Are you developing skills now to have an equal partnership in the future?

3. VALUE DIFFERENCES IN FAMILY MEMBERS

If we look at the variety of human beings' talents, looks, tastes, and so on, it is clear that our Heavenly Mother and Heavenly Father value differences. When They looked upon the earth with its diverse creations, They called it **good**. So how does this apply to your family? Each person's uniqueness should be recognized and celebrated. After all, we'll be spending a lot of time (eternity) together!

LIFE TIP: Those who have been rejected by their earthly families, who have suffered from parents' choices, or who might never be able to marry can find comfort knowing that they are sealed to Heavenly Parents who will love them ALWAYS. All can find love, joy, and belonging in the FAMILY of heaven.

 Ephesians 3:10–17

Come back and
record your
experiences
speaking of
Heavenly Mother
in church:

_____

_____

_____

_____

_____

_____

_____

_____

_____

_____

_____

_____

Artist:
David Cassler,
She Returns

IN YOUR CHURCH COMMUNITY

The Church of Jesus Christ's website says, "The doctrine of a Heavenly Mother is a cherished and distinctive belief among Latter-day Saints."

So let's celebrate this truth!

Next time you give a talk in church or a lesson in family study, include your Heavenly Mother. When appropriate, bring Her up in Sunday School discussions. Sing songs that praise Her and Heavenly Father (such as hymns 286, 292, and 311). When your heart swells within you to bear testimony, speak eternal truths regarding your Heavenly Parents. Follow examples of Church leaders who have spoken of Heavenly Mother...like these:

CREATE CHANGE #3

66 I testify of loving Heavenly Parents; of our Savior, Jesus Christ; and of His infinite Atonement in our behalf. 99

– President Linda K. Burton

66 When we return to our real home, it will be with the 'mutual approbation' of those who reign in the 'royal courts on high.' There we will find beauty such as mortal 'eye hath not seen'; we will hear sounds of surpassing music which mortal 'ear hath not heard.' Could such a regal homecoming be possible without the anticipatory arrangements of a Heavenly Mother? 99

– Elder Neal A. Maxwell

66 Men and women together have a Godlike status, for the Lord said male and female created he them in his own image. Some have questioned our concept of a mother in heaven, but no home, no church, no heaven would be complete without a mother there. 99

– Elder Hugh B. Brown

THROUGHOUT THE WHOLE WORLD

Prophets teach what the world needs to hear. And we are supposed to make that truth come alive in the world!

CREATE CHANGE #4

> Apostle Neal A. Maxwell taught, "In this dispensation the Lord gave us this doctrinal truth [of Heavenly Mother] through a prophet...The basic truths are always the same, but the emphasis needed will be made by living prophets under inspiration from the living God, and the people of the living Church will respond."

Why is the truth of Heavenly Mother so needed in our time? Just take a look around...

1. KNOWING OF OUR HEAVENLY MOTHER TELLS US HOW ALL WOMEN SHOULD BE TREATED.

All over the world, women are often discriminated against. With restored doctrine, we know that Heavenly Mother and Heavenly Father are partners—and earthly relationships, policies, and practices should mirror that! So when we look at all our earthly sisters (those in your family and all those around you), let us see in them a reflection of our Heavenly Mother. Let us seek their viewpoints, cherish their wisdom, and appreciate their differences.

2. KNOWING OF OUR HEAVENLY MOTHER MEANS THE DEFINITION OF MOTHERHOOD IS EXPANDED.

Mothering, based on the model of Heavenly Mother, is literally as large and inclusive as the universe. Earthly mothers can do their best to love and nurture their children...but there are many, many ways to go about that! Respect different ways of mothering.

3. KNOWING OF OUR HEAVENLY MOTHER MEANS WE UNDERSTAND WE ARE PART OF A HEAVENLY FAMILY.

Our Heavenly Parents are EVERYONE'S parents! They created and celebrate difference. Let's discard our prejudices to see all as wonderfully unique and equal siblings. As Sister Chieko N. Okazaki said: —

 HOW DO YOU THINK THE WORLD WOULD BE BETTER IF WE HONORED OUR HEAVENLY MOTHER AND ALL OF HER DAUGHTERS? WHAT CAN YOU DO TO HELP?

Artist: Brooke Bowen, *Heavenly Mother Feeding Manna to Her Children*

66 Each of us is on a quest in this life to purify ourselves of mists and veils so that we may see truly and clearly into each other's hearts and there perceive that each one is a sister or a brother, equally a beloved child of our loving Heavenly Parents. 99

– Sister Chieko N. Okazaki

LIFE TIP: Remember all are children of Heavenly Parents. You sing "I am a child of God" but remember—"he or she too is a child of God"—and grasp your responsibility to all people as your brothers and sisters!

WELCOME HOME!

Remember how Heavenly Father introduced Jesus Christ in the Sacred Grove? "This is my Beloved Son, in whom I am well pleased."

Won't it be amazing to hear those same words spoken of you?

Your Heavenly Mother and Heavenly Father WANT you to come back to Them. Remember, They love you. They will help you. Stay close to Them... and return home in glory.

HYMN #286, "Oh, What Songs of the Heart," talks about that time:

"Oh, what songs we'll employ!
Oh, what welcome we'll hear!
While our transports of love are complete,
As the heart swells with joy
In embraces most dear
When our heavenly parents we meet!"

---

66 You are here on a mission and in a few years you will 'be released' to go home to Father and Mother to 'give an account of your labors, to tell your experiences' and what you have accomplished on the earth. How proud our parents are of a son who has filled an honorable mission! With what joy they welcome him home! 99

— Matilda E. Teasdale

66 What! to meet, besides my Father in heaven, a Mother also? The thought thrills my whole being with an inexpressible joy. What a wealth of beauty and grandeur the thought adds to my conceptions of God and heaven. 99

— Nephi L. Anderson

Artist: Linda V. Etherington, *Mother in Heaven*

45

ACTIVITY PAGES

There are lots of ways you can develop your testimony of Heavenly Mother. Below are a few. Enjoy!

THINK

What advice would your Heavenly Mother give you?

_____
_____
_____
_____
_____
_____
_____
_____
_____
_____
_____
_____
_____
_____
_____
_____
_____
_____

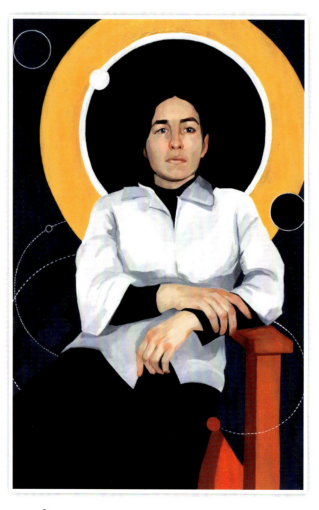

← Artist: Allen Tenbusschen, *Creations*

READ

Ponder these scriptures and consider how they become more meaningful knowing you have a Heavenly Mother:

Genesis 1:1–2; 26–27

Deuteronomy 32:11–12; 18

Isaiah 42:14

Isaiah 66:13

Hosea 11:3–4

Hosea 13:8

Psalm 57:1; 139:13

Matthew 3:17

Matthew 17:5

Luke 3:22

Luke 13:34

1 Nephi 21:15

3 Nephi 10:4–6

Abraham 4:27

DRAW

Create a picture of Heavenly Mother. And, if you want, email it to seekingheavenlymother@gmail.com and they will post your art in their permanent collection online and maybe on their social media!

IMAGINE

Put on a pair of imaginary glasses. Pretend these glasses make you see the world as our Heavenly Parents see it. How is this different from how you normally see the world? Does it change how you see your family? Strangers? The earth around you? Record your thoughts here:

_____

_____

_____

_____

_____

_____

_____

_____

MOVE

Consider how your body is a gift from our Heavenly Parents. And go use it!

→ **Run/jog/walk** a mile.

→ **Jump rope** for two minutes.

→ **Run stairs**—how many times can you go up and down a flight in one minute?

→ **Sprint** three times to the mailbox (or something) and time yourself. Can you beat your time?

→ **Ride your bike** for twenty minutes and see how far you can go.

→ How far can you **throw a frisbee**?

→ Can you **balance a coin** on your nose?

Learn and record information about your female ancestors. Consider not just their names, but also their occupations and what they loved, endured, sacrificed, witnessed, and looked like. Write down what you find. How are you like them? How are they like Heavenly Mother?

Mother

Name:

Occupation:

Passions:

Events Witnessed:

Made Her Happy:

Sacrifices Made:

Grandmothers

Name:

Occupation:

Passions:

Events Witnessed:

Sacrifices Made:

- - - - - - - - - - - - -

Name:

Occupation:

Passions:

Events Witnessed:

Sacrifices Made:

Great-Grandmothers

Name:

Occupation:

Passions:

Sacrifices Made:

- - - - - - - - - - - - -

Name:

Occupation:

Passions:

Sacrifices Made:

- - - - - - - - - - - - -

Name:

Occupation:

Passions:

Sacrifices Made:

- - - - - - - - - - - - -

Name:

Occupation:

Passions:

Sacrifices Made:

McArthur Krishna

Life is a gift from our Heavenly Parents—a grand, demanding, insane adventure. Along the way, McArthur has worked as a window washer, a construction crew member, an archeological aid, a Bollywood extra, a river rafting guide, a business owner, an artist. Those adventures led to publishing seventeen children's books (including four with Deseret Book) and new job titles—Holy Harasser and Hogwash Eradicator. Now, she travels the world with her family and dreams of West Virginia rivers, zydeco dancing, and bottomless guacamole.

Martin Pulido

Businessman by day, father of three by night, and writer and scholar by late night, Martin juggles roles while living in the grassy, northern plains of the Lone Star State. He has written and spoken extensively on Heavenly Mother in academic settings, and co-authored the seminal *BYU Studies'* article "'A Mother There': A Survey of Historical Teachings about Mother in Heaven," which informed the official Church's gospel topics essay "Mother in Heaven." Thereafter, Martin organized the A Mother Here: Art and Poetry Contest. Material generated from that contest, and much historical research, formed the basis for the award-winning *Dove Song: Heavenly Mother in Mormon Poetry*, of which Martin was co-editor and contributor.

Artist: Emilie Buck Lewis, *All Can Be Like unto God*

Bethany Brady Spalding

Bethany focuses her life on family, faith, feminism, and good food and wild fun for all! Many of these passions have come together to co-author five children's books with McArthur—including *A Girl's Guide to Heavenly Mother*.

References

Page 2: John H. Vandenberg, "In Search of Truth," *Improvement Era*, June 1970, 59.

Russell M. Nelson, in Janet Peterson's, "Friend to Friend: From a Personal Interview by Janet Peterson with Elder Russell M. Nelson of the Quorum of the Twelve," *Friend*, Jan. 1986.

Pages 6-7: James E. Talmage, "The Philosophical Basis of 'Mormonism,'" *Improvement Era*, Sept. 1915, 950.

Dallin H. Oaks, "Apostasy and Restoration," *Ensign*, May 1995.

John A. Widtsoe, "Editorial: Everlasting Motherhood," *Millennial Star*, May 1928, 298.

Pages 8-9: Franklin D. Richards and James E. Little, *A Compendium of the Doctrines of the Gospel* (Salt Lake City: Deseret News Company, 1882), 118–19.

M. Russell Ballard, "Return and Receive," *Ensign*, May 2017.

Pages 10-11: Susa Young Gates, "The Vision Beautiful," *Improvement Era*, Apr. 1920, 542–43.

Bryant S. Hinckley, *Sermons and Missionary Services of Melvin J. Ballard* (Salt Lake City: Deseret Book Company, 1949), 205.

Pages 12-13: Elaine A. Cannon, "Mother in Heaven," in *The Encyclopedia of Mormonism* (New York: Macmillan, 1992), 961.

Pages 14-15: Gary E. Stevenson, "Blessings of a Gospel Perspective," *Liahona*, Oct. 2019.

Ronald A. Rasband, "Lest Thou Forget," *Ensign*, Nov. 2016.

Spencer W. Kimball, "Privileges and Responsibilities of Sisters," *Ensign*, Nov. 1978.

Pages 16-17: Orson F. Whitney, "We Walk by Faith," *Improvement Era*, May 1916, 609.

Pages 18-19: Jeffrey R. Holland and Patricia T. Holland, *On Earth as It Is in Heaven* (Salt Lake City: Deseret Book Company, 1989), 4.

Pages 22-23: Thomas S. Monson, "Ponder the Path of Thy Feet," *Ensign*, Nov. 2014.

Pages 24-25: Henry B. Eyring, "The Family," in *To Draw Closer to God: A Collection of Discourses* (Salt Lake City: Deseret Book Company, 1997), 160–61.

Pages 26-27: Jeffrey R. Holland, "Behold Thy Mother," *Ensign*, Nov. 2015.

Vaughn J. Featherstone, "A Champion of Youth," *Ensign*, Nov. 1987.

Pages 28-29: Susa Young Gates, "Boy Versus Girl," *The Young Woman's Journal*, Oct. 1894, 31–32.

B. H. Roberts, "The Church of Jesus Christ of Latter-day Saints at the Parliament of Religions: V. Woman's Place in 'Mormonism,'" *Improvement Era*, Oct. 1899, 900.

Pages 30–31: M. Russell Ballard, "To Whom Shall We Go?," *Ensign*, Nov. 2016.

Jeffrey R. Holland, "Be Ye Therefore Perfect—Eventually," *Ensign*, Nov. 2017.

Pages 32-33: John Taylor, "Man," in *Journal of Discourses*, 8 (London: Latter-day Saints' Book Depot, 1860), 4–5.

Pages 34-35: Francine R. Bennion, "A Latter-day Saint Theology of Suffering," in Jennifer Reeder and Kate Holbrook, eds., *At the Pulpit: 185 Years of Discourses by Latter-day Saint Women* (Salt Lake City: Deseret Book Company, 2017), 217.

Pages 38-39: David C. Kimball, "Reflections on the Destiny of Man," *Millennial Star*, June 1846, 184.

Pages 40–41: Linda K. Burton, "Certain Women," *Ensign*, May 2017.

Hugh B. Brown, *Continuing the Quest* (Salt Lake City: Deseret Book Company, 1961), 8.

Neal A. Maxwell, "Women of God," *Ensign*, May 1978.

Pages 42–43: Neal A. Maxwell, *Things as They Really Are* (Salt Lake City: Deseret Book Company, 1978), 67.

Chieko N. Okazaki, *Sanctuary* (Salt Lake City: Deseret Book Company, 1997), 57.

Pages 44–45: Matilda E. Teasdale, "To the Young Ladies of Zion," *The Young Woman's Journal*, July 1892, 472.

Nephi L. Anderson, "A Little Visit to Glory-Land," *Millennial Star*, Sept. 1905, 562–63.

Additional resources can be found here:

- LDS Gospel Essay on Mother in Heaven: www.churchofjesuschrist.org/study/manual/gospel-topics-essays/mother-in-heaven?lang=eng

- David Paulsen and Martin Pulido's article "'A Mother There': A Survey of Historical Teachings about Mother in Heaven," published by BYU Studies: www.byustudies.byu.edu/content/mother-there-survey-historical-teachings-about-mother-heaven

- www.SeekingHeavenlyMother.com

- McArthur Krishna and Bethany Brady Spalding's book: *Heavenly Family, Earthly Families* by Deseret Book

- Elaine Anderson Cannon. "Mother in Heaven." Encyclopedia of Mormonism. 1992. "Becoming like God." ChurchofJesusChrist.org, February 2014, www.churchofjesuschrist.org/study/manual/gospel-topics-essays/becoming-like-god

Artist: Stephanie Northrup, *Are We Not All Beggars III*

Dedications

To My Boys—I imagine if Heavenly Mother were here, She would spend many hours holding you close and reminding you that you are going to do great things with your mind, body, and talents. She would probably nourish you with lots of good food and good books. She would run with you, wrestle you, and jump off big rocks into the water with you. She would help you overcome your fears and be your biggest cheerleader. She would be the ultimate example of compassion, empathy, and service. She would listen to you and you would desire to be near Her and stand in awe with gratitude. I hope this book gives you even just a glimmer of what that could someday be like.

– McArthur Krishna (thanks to Amber)

To my Mothers and sons,
and a Church I love

– Martin Pulido

To my brilliant nephew, Zach—the first boy to crack open my heart and teach me how to love with gusto!

– Bethany Brady Spalding

Thank you to:

For their editing, Tracy Keck & Ashley Stahle

For fabulous graphic design and layout,
Kate Purcell—www.katepurcell.com

 D Street PRESS

Text copyrighted by D Street Press. All illustration rights are owned by individual artists. First published in USA by D Street Press in 2020. For information about permission to reproduce selections from the book, write howdy@dstreetpress.com.

D Street Press, Portland, OR, 97239 USA. Printed in India.

ISBN 978-1-7342287-1-7

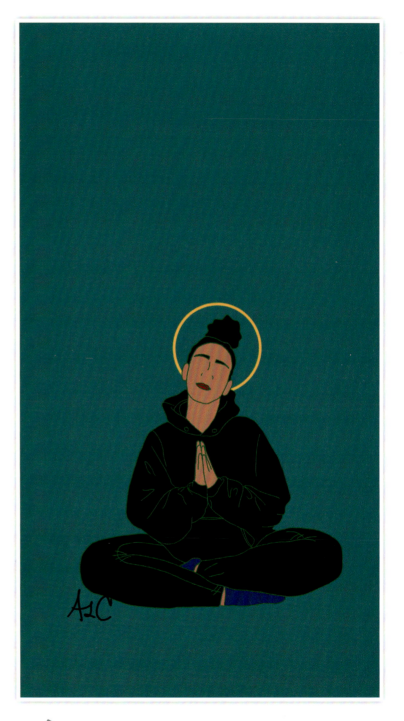

Artist: Ashly S. Correia, *Heavenly Mother*